Prayers for Bobby

∞ ∞ ∞

Jamie Shaw

SWEETSPIRE **LITERATURE**
——— MANAGEMENT ———

for Jade

God made you, Jade, so sweet,
You make me thirst, to taste
The nectar of you, neat
In poem, prayer, and paste †

When Topaz was my colour,
Garnet made some room for Jade:
Nirvana, here in summer—
Best move Heaven ever made †

The man in me, a rogue, a rover,
Weeps to keep his love in check—
To be a lover never over,
Love in time his **szeretlek** †

Part One:

"Let there be Love..."

If Love is my answer,
Her heart is my quest—
The loveliest dancer
Doth beat in her breast:

She saves me when loss comes,
She saves me from me—
The sweetest of possums,
So beauteously

Bequeathing her breathing,
From which I, in zeal,
Shall ever be leaving
Impressions I feel,

As, melting inside us,
Two hearts, fill'd with joy,
In hopes hale guide us:
One girl—and her boy.

'Anna'

[one]

She pits a wispy black moustache
To complement her till
With inner eyes, where hope is harsh
For banking on a kill!
Her silence makes a gentle prod
Too beautiful to bear:
She must believe a mental god
Is driven to despair—
To count on love, when love purloins
The lint above her lip
In preference to the notes he coins
In giving her the slip...
True: thirty years, or thirty-one,
Remember her this way;
To tell her so, is time undone,
Or merely here to stay?

'Elie'

[two]

At war with peace today predates,
He interposes night—
To balance checks before he mates
Contrition with delight!
His essence is a battle fought,
A cataclysm wed
To sons of sorrow selling short
The Bibles in his head...
A sea of placid beauty, such
As pits upon the Moon,
Might end up in a sister's touch
Her brothers will impugn—
For sure as zig begins to zag,
We are one people who
Believe the bull and knot the rag
Blood-red and wrung *adieu*!

'Heidi'

[three]

A second back, about to come,
She settles on a place
Where ice, in short supply for some,
May land the Human Race!
And yet she is still here for me—
Within my head a dove,
To win a whirring fantasy
And counsel me in love,
Confers on Christmas conifers
The mistletoe and myrrh
Apparent to the monitors
Superior to her...
As, wan, I wonder, wait, and watch,
To be her luck or lunch—
A bore is game to bait and botch
Her funky succour punch!

'Guy'

[four]

A big fish in a little pond?
Recant your blasphemy!
You'd posit one of willing wand
To curb his majesty:
But contradict the hypocrite,
Then annotate the Lie,
To blitz men in the grip of it—
Or, failing that, to try;
And he will spill his wit in words
Like flowers at your feet:
Ranunculi for pretty birds,
Potatoes for their meat...
For he is like a fisher, not
The one to fall for bait;
Each brilliant *coup*, each crushing *shot*,
Is *force majeure*—Checkmate!

'Avigail'

[five]

If I could count your richest gain
And be what he prefers,
I'd wrap for you in cellophane
Liaisons dangereuses...
Your Hebrew soul, your hair of black,
Your skin of perfect brown—
L'chaim, love, to life come back,
Abdominal in down!
Pray, whither did your spirit fly?
Did David's mandolin
Escort you quiet waters by?
Your waterworks within
Have made of me the fool for drops
A weeping *kosher* glove
Dispersed through rough and ready crops—
To irrigate your love!

'Merlin'

[six]

She wishes me more merriment
Than truth could hope to bear,
Were Heaven not more Heaven-sent
Considering her there:
Am I her man, or love to burn,
More flickering than flame?
If I see ashes in her urn,
Remembering to tame
Long years of wonder at her dance,
Felicity and mirth,
Devotion flirting with romance
That heralds its rebirth—
Protect me from the Gates of Hell,
Not seeing her beside,
Until I crush her magic spell
Exonerating pride.

'Lucky'

[seven]

El Lute wasn't quite as odd
As *clérigos* in teams
Tridentical—content to plod
In continental seams
Nigh hot enough to simmer guts
Gestating in her brew:
The tea before the billy shuts
Rosacea in a mew
Elusive as the waterlilies
Asking eyes to stare
Complicity, as mortar shimmies
Lustre on repair…
Except to say: it burns and burns,
Until it burns no more;
Perhaps it comes and then returns—
Seclusion for the poor.

'Misha'

[eight]

Congratulations—on your work,
The genius of love:
Conceptions lesser beings shirk
When passion comes above
Intransigence so brutal, yes,
Though brilliant as the sea
That twinkles with your watercress
For rivulets of glee...
Rehearsals—that is what I strove,
Hereditary, in awe,
To emulate, as though a stove
Unable to ignore
The cluster of the cardamom
Upon the golden meat,
The little waves that ebb and strum
Above their silver beet.

'Tiger'

[nine]

A kitten's on the welling stairs,
Companion over time
Thought much too short for Knights or Mares—
Purrfection in its prime!
I wonder where she wanders through—
On hills as green and young
As jade emporia I knew
When innocence still clung...
The scent of her, my sweet sarong
To buy and not to sell,
Is less a cushion, more a prong
Than aspic is for gel—
If love goes on, if love is free,
If passion has a say;
The one I do still love is she—
Or hope to, yesterday.

'Jacqui'

[ten]

I stutter, thinking of her far
Too far from such as me;
This morning moon's an evening star
For relativity
Disproven: if she's coming back,
Lest love be lost, akin
To making up for colour's lack
In palaces we pin
With light caressing me and her
I feel lurk upon
Thy prepossessing shield, Sir,
When Heaven's daughter's gone...
So let me hope to love again
And I shall love repay—
Like Daniel in the Lions' Den,
Inclining, come what may.

'Gretel'

[eleven]

She's much too odd to be so—even
In the light of day;
If you need someone to believe in
(In your disarray)
Be sure to check her equinox:
A hand of solitaire
Too radiant, too heterodox,
To dwindle into air...
There is a problem being one:
Except for human touch,
There's nothing left, when all is done,
That heals quite as much
Along the way for truth in life
She's poking into view—
Whose candle flickers through my strife
Too promising for two.

'Esther'

[twelve]

She's hard to lose, but he won't play
The Morning Star—I quote;
If virtue is an honest *trait*,
Concession is a coat
For other idols, open wide
To hallowing her shape,
Transposing wetlands into pride
From which he can't escape...
His songbird it is mine to be:
To serenade a fox
That man in me contends to see
Refuting aftershocks,
I bite on granite, light as air,
To counterbalance dark
Predisposition for the fair
Birds of a feather—hark!

'Fisch'

[thirteen]

Yet not his will, but mine be done
On Earth, if not above:
Division's catholic for the nun
Superior in love—
Lest, looking lonesome to the sky,
She hold his handkerchief,
On trial for whose do or die
We chorus unbelief...
So hoping not to open it,
I bleed my fix of sap,
Quite at a loss to cope in it—
That unfamiliar trap
That makes of life a *maelstrom*,
Of love a refugee
Meowing for her doubting tom
Who pins her to his tree.

'Whinny'

[fourteen]

Her wisdom seeps through Heaven's cracks—
In God Almighty's view
Her starry, starry Knight attacks
The troubadours in you
Who judge the juries who prepare
To sac a son and sob
Acute inclusion of your prayer
In reveries we rob...
Say *szeretlek*, I love you, hon—
The citizens of Earth
May take a pill, may take a gun
To Hell, for what it's worth—
But you're the kind of frenemy
I'd sooner underrate
Than sweethearts, in defence of me,
I check before I mate.

'Shelley'

[fifteen]

My heart is beating as it skips
Across a frank *fjord*—
I pander to placental lips
Once amorously moored
En garde before a night too dark
To make the time of day
Consensual with Heaven's park
Beyond her sweet array...
Admittance thither, into her,
Inviting me to come—
As though her sole intention were
To send resistance numb—
Will make of loss a little less,
The *Lieder* somehow grave,
If her religion is to bless
And I'm the one to save!

'Garfelia'

[sixteen]

A shadow in my brain, on pause,
Meowing for her tom—
The little lover on all fours,
As purrs profess aplomb—
Takes refuge in less evident
Emergence from today's
Delirium: such merriment
That fills as it decays...
My little girl, I pray for you:
Your singular's the most
My love can be—if I am to
Bejewel whom I toast,
I'll hear your heart, I'll sigh for sight,
To treasure at the end
Love's *saboteur* conferring light
Upon a stirring friend.

'Janis'

[seventeen]

If God is where you shouldn't be,
His wish is my command:
One set of eyes I long to see
May be His sleight of hand—
To whisk your breath and body thence
And, leaving not a trace,
Grant solace in unholy sense
No being can replace...
You learnt the truth: the hand of God's
Too fickle for His foes;
Exactly whom the Land of Nod's
Expecting, Heaven knows—
But when you ponder how she purrs
Inside you, as she sleeps,
Remember how your likes and hers
Are never meant for keeps!

'Manny'

[eighteen]

You'd think I'd know just who you are—
The pirate on the plank
Meanders like a stolen car
To burst the bit I bank
On champing at, as rivers come
In sadness I construe
To see deception's merit plumb
Unfathomable you...
So who am I to spark your flame?
To hire you a mo
The man you are a man became
Unbeatably my foe:
But womankind has love to spread
And proves it with her thighs—
Perhaps she needs her noggin read
By you, or other lies!

'Ruby'

[nineteen]

You're so above me, so beyond
Synopsis, like a waltz
That woos a tired vagabond
And infiltrates his pulse:
Enable me to trade in men,
To capture whom I please—
Their elegy's a pathogen
Rewritten on your breeze—
As pins and puns fill up my lungs
With pride, before the fall
Of mediocre speech in tongues
Now coming back to maul...
Yet one upon my heart is sweet
As ever sunshine knew
Could make its friendly fire heat
Incalculably you!

'Taylor'

[twenty]

She's thirty-four and popular
As God at thirty-three:
It seems no one can stop to star
On top of Heaven's tree
As shakily as she does—though
If God were still in town,
He'd tell her not to bleed, as *beaux*
Escorting her renown...
My love, she's priceless, as you were,
The very best there was,
For whom my prose, so amateur,
Is *kibitzing*—because
In orisons I say "I do",
Though many say "I did":
Like thwarted orphans nodding to
Caïssa's only kid.

'Sheila'

[twenty-one]

Forgive me, Lord, for I have sinned—
To covet is a crime
More enigmatic than the wind
That buries it in rhyme...
It takes a lot to lose, perfuse
Compassion with contempt;
So maybe it's not mine to choose,
Nor mine to be exempt:
Her loveliness has cast a spell—
To offer up like gold
The scintillating way to Hell
For those who won't be told...
So I am hers, if not the first
To weep with gnashing teeth—
At worst, athirst, to be immersed,
Love welling from her heath!

'Goldilocks'

[twenty-two]

She's standing on the corner, far
From fortune, far from fame;
If, caught in candour, we debar
The *chugger* she became,
She'll smell as sweet amidst the thorns
Complicit in pizazz
For witchery on wistful lawns
One rhododendron has...
I'll be her chill *conquistador*,
Her apple and her dew—
I wonder what her world is for,
Or what it's coming to—
If locks of gold are worth my plugs,
If, taken to the task,
Her hirsute heroism hugs
My meretricious mask!

'Pete'

[twenty-three]

Go easy on me, *Monsignor*,
Your love is warm as toast;
You peddle poor *esprit de corps*
Of which *compadres* boast
In parables of Heaven's hold
Upon the meek and glum:
I'm told your mould is rolled in gold
For giving in—how come?
If death must be, long live the first:
The seconds come and go
For subterraneans immersed
In catatonic woe
Too never-ending—conscience pricks
My eyes upon the prize
Whose game lives on the crucifix
So hard to equalize.

'Josephine'

[twenty-four]

I look to find her looking snide—
Her garden bed deters
The Jekyll in my Mr Hyde
From taking what is hers
And, banking on her rainy days,
Investing every scent
Belonging to her castaways
In irises we lent...
The present spends what history earns
But here I am, somehow,
The ivy climbing over ferns
That came and went: a *ciao*
Too fond to squander spunk, address
The plots too hot to see—
Without whose blessing I finesse
Proclivity for me!

'Chris'

[twenty-five]

Surprisingly like spirit spliced—
That's how he comes to me
Reshouldering his holy heist:
A sow's redundancy
Caressing hope, parading hurt,
To chasten spite ablaze
With ire, keeping faith alert
For grace that might amaze...
But what if, just a lonely bum,
He's not as white as snow?
If, furthermore, the Lord is come
For breaking up below
The choir and the cabalist,
Who, succour for a stone,
Will twist their gist to coexist
On God's forsaken throne?

'Wolfie'

[twenty-six]

As noble as come fishing rods

To stalk primeval fronds—

Sweet peas in pods that care how God's

Existence corresponds—

I scour Hell and Heaven, more

Conspirator than friend:

For who can see, and not adore,

Illusion without end?

So many lines, so many clues—

Can anyone emerge

From light that blinds, in hope that woos,

The prayers a dramaturge

Assembles? Take the stars on high

That twinkle in defence

Of faith—so welcome to the sky,

Though ignorant of whence!

'Rachael'

[twenty-seven]

If you were mine, and love to make,
I'd drink you like liqueur:
Martinis, in your tender wake,
Proprietrix of fur,
Are stirring in my wishing well—
If fire can be met
By ducking duty's citadel
Too brutal to regret,
Perfection is persuasive, yes,
I put that curse on you:
So much more than a game of Chess,
A mate in three or two...
If therefore I must fail, wait—
It is my turn to move:
True love shall be the stalemate
That draws on Heaven's groove!

'Abby'

[twenty-eight]

So much for women—give me hope
That I repay design
To overreach your isotope
In gambits we decline!
Allow me to ingratiate
This posy in my soul—
If parts of me emaciate
The quotient of your whole,
'Tis list relit that lifts your veil,
Baring beauty hid
Astride bewitchment of the Grail
Whence desire slid...
So let us make of supper, love,
Collation for the Moon—
Who, sensing starlight up above,
Embroils it as soon?

'Barney'

[twenty-nine]

The long and winding avenue
Wound up forevermore
To see you masterminding to
Achieve an even score...
"I let you mate me!" yes, you did—
You didn't miss a move;
I'm trying hard to keep a lid
On nothing left to prove:
For you are still the Champion—
No matter what my sieve
Lets filter through, the lamp is on
The luminance you give
To whisperings and images
Explaining in my head
Exactly who the winner is
Whom lachrymation shed.

'Zoë'

[thirty]

Is woman kind? Does butter fly?
Does winning take the cake?
Is Everest still there, so high
Above that greasy lake
That takes your hope and pins it down:
On fire, in despair,
You're asking God to let you drown—
Your novelty in prayer?
She's life, and yes: she's ever kind,
The wench I chance to choose;
She's like Caïssa, less resigned
To be the lass I lose—
Than soothe my savage breast, collect
First fruits I felt in glove:
Her King is hurting, still erect,
And face to face, in love.

'Georgia'

[thirty-one]

Your apparition's pull, so plush,
Produces such supreme
Dystopia, we've got a crush
On killers born to steam
Like *haricots*—to pay your price
Can't leave us better off
Than all the others eating icy
Follicles you doff...
Hop home, as heinous hoods whore on
To hook and hang and hew—
Though vile is, and best forgone,
The shock they rock into—
Which waits, as wailing walls of woe,
On heroes who just aren't
Unbeatable—though not as Joe
You'd better, but you can't!

'Honey'

[thirty-two]

Good Lord, why can't you save me too?
You're saving up yourself
For making crumbs in gravy brew
To sate an avid elf...
Is eight enough? Those chicken legs
Do justice to your eyes:
Preponderant as wire pegs
That spin for little flies...
So tough a teddy—take the stairs!—
Who wipes away the stains?—
My God, you're born to run for prayers
And sundry other gains...
How great you are—to skip across,
Entrusting spruce to pine:
Hot dogs will dig the way you're boss,
But quake to be divine!

'Betty'

[thirty-three]

They speculate, but what is love
If I'm averse to her?
We'll ache a little more, to shove
Her bootylicious burr
On up into Plutonic peaks
As, champing at the bit,
Her choirs crackle as she creaks,
Eponymous as spit…
My heroine, extraneous
For adamantine ways—
Deluxe production waning plus
Kaleidoscopic glaze—
Can sink her suitors, as she slips,
Like rubbers in a band:
Need lemonade? Squeeze lemon pips—
Bandanas on demand!

'Master'

[thirty-four]

To be, though true, the cream your crop
Bewitches—dynasties
Of *pick-me-ups* on jaws I drop,
Angelic by degrees—
May prepossess your pedestal
Generic for the ones
Like you and me, who rise and fall
With callisthenic suns...
Hey, can't you see our chopper? Mate,
It's time for us to land—
Sure, poppies discombobulate
Red circles in the sand
For making love inscrutable,
Evolving as a trade:
Pituitaries immutable
Drink cognac in the shade!

'Margot'

[thirty-five]

I met you when I met regret
A little later on;
Forgive me if I let your debt
See fit to wait upon
Proclivity to leap and lope
In blossoming of bliss
Found wanting—like the dawn of Hope
You mask before you miss...
So just like me to go for gals
To obviate divorce
On counterfeit diagonals
We're heralding till, hoarse,
It turns out, like true opposites,
Your heart lights up the dark,
As I am left to shop for wit's
Episcopal remark!

'Gemma'

[thirty-six]

Such loveliness she's waking in
My being—wanting hers
To be the mare I'm breaking in
With fire-breathing spurs
Devotedly I'm burying
In fond and faithful flanks
Whose yesterdays are just the thing
On which her morrow banks:
She up and left before I came
To stroke and, to her pull,
Compose the country, frame by frame,
About her cotton wool—
So sue me if I go too far
In thinking her the best:
Inside my soul I see her—thar
She blows, at my behest!

'Amália'

thirty-seven

How then was yours an open door
More *con* than any *pro*?
Erotic law you can't ignore
But, going with the flow,
You hit me with a glancing shock
I thought at first a shot:
Your legacy's a cuckoo clock
Whom time concedes not what
You, quizzical coquette, in kind,
Pandora's Box to ope,
Rate roses of regret resigned
To passion's slippery slope...
Grand Mistress, your tiara's on,
To ratify your claim
To have the edge—if love is wan
Enough to lose your game!

'Carla'

[thirty-eight]

To catch your soul, a lambent lap
Lets compensation sigh
For insurrection—quell the tap
That's got it getting high!
Now, to this mind, you're ever young,
And I not so much less—
Do you still know my mouth and tongue
In toe to your caress?
I'm wondering if you exist
For family, friends, and God—
Will you still answer if I twist
Your arm, to give the nod
To one condoning love and loss
Which can't diminish you?
I'm lichen clinging to your moss,
So happy that it grew!

'Ella'

[thirty-nine]

I look across her window's lens
To see her doing time;
If, thinking of her, prudence pens
Compassion for her crime,
'Tis never nice to miss a check,
For checks can end in mates—
And, in a madhouse, what the heck,
Who isn't loving, hates...
They share a birthday, she and God;
If Jesus is for freaks,
She's with him in her holy bod
And sanity that leaks—
When supermodels push ahead
If they're not pushing wood;
A case in point: her sunshine bled
Or she's misunderstood!

'Ronald'

[forty]

His Moses wrote dictations down
On tablets: unlike his
Promotion of the thorny crown
Embellishing that whiz
For whom he prays in litanies
Apportioning despair—
If only craven wit agrees
That's worthy of a prayer!
Hoe in, my friend, but don't forget
Almighty God enslaves
Nomadic Pawns—if His gazette
Depicts how *manna* saves,
Lay Pharaoh, knowing when to punch
Or how to duck, concurs:
Veracity has got a hunch
Enlightenment prefers!

'Hug'

[forty-one]

If you are gone, still I remain
To search for searching's sake;
Where you were King, pretenders reign
As variations snake
Both left in love and right in ruth
For someone lost to men
And women—wanting wilting youth
To come to life again...
Let Heaven open for its guest
And let him not resign
Himself, though in the wild west
A lonely ball may shine—
For still I love, and you are whom
Caïssa's calling Lord:
You size them up, as flowers bloom
Like lovers, over board.

'Kathryn'

[forty-two]

The fragrance of her bloom will stay
Tomorrow in my heart—
If yesterday is on the way
To pull today apart,
Where is my rose, except in dreams?
For yes, she yonder dwells—
She is the one devotion schemes
To buy up if she sells...
So many years I took her spark
To wed a beating chest
With daylight in the crescent dark
Of moonbeams on a quest
To cast in ink the fading hope
Her soul will bind to mine—
Lest faith in loveliness elope
And list so disincline!

'Yaniv, GM'

[forty-three]

If I'm a legend, what of *him*
To whom we tender love?
For others now 'tis growing dim
But fire like a dove
Is burning in my cheated chest—
To see him as he is
Through eyes which view the best by test
As lucidly as his...
My friend, how were you, so to speak,
So best? To meet your match
You let my resignation seek
To tie you down, then snatch
Redemption from a *Ruy Lopez*
Not even God's defence
Indents—like *Señor Ajedrez*
Against omnipotence!

'Chantelle'

[forty-four]

If, at the going down of love
And in the morning light,
I wear her distance like a glove
On skin once nearly white,
Is sweet surrender ceding there
Improvements in design—
Inclined to bear what I despair
To see confessing mine?
I thank the Lord, for, OMG,
He saved me yet again
From fixing love for show, when the
Majority of men
Are sensible to woman's wile
Lurking like a kite
Imponderable as chamomile
Capturing the night.

'Howard'

[forty-five]

Your peace, too hard to understand,
In poetry I stage
Each time my truant hinterland
Consoles a silent page...
The Knight—so noble, so abstruse;
The Bishop—clean and true;
The Queen—so free when on the loose;
The King—I think of you:
If Shakespeare had his scholar, there
In England mourning thorns
Bereft of roses—*debonair*
As lionhearted Pawns,
You're pressing on into the light:
Somewhere beyond my ken
You are my Rook, if Black is White—
And birds shall rule again!

'Sarah'

[forty-six]

You look so good—I'd like to sup
On you, if but to see
The way your jeans are giving up
Divertissement for me!
Some say that souls are for the ear
More so than for the eye:
If so, your optics volunteer
For love I simplify
To picturesque commotion, when,
Chevalier in deep,
Phantasmagoria's the glen
Through which libidos leap...
So, let your body's cotton wing
Be silent as the curves
I sketch—as such a blossoming
Phenomenon deserves!

'Judith'

[forty—seven]

Quite Heavenly, yes: quite a Queen,
Not lacking any knack
For conjuring, while still a teen,
A win—with White or Black!
If you were born a Princess, sworn
To pressure flesh enmeshed
Each time a Knight would pin your lawn
To Buda &/or Pest,
Do you not wish Caïssa's Prince
Besought Caïssa's Maid
To love, like zesty peppermints,
The brilliancies you trade?
For he, the best there ever was,
Might well have met his match
In you—the best there is, because
His plot's got what you hatch!

'Virginia'

[forty-eight]

Forever young—at least back then,
When time for us was new:
I put my periscopic pen
To paper for the dew
That twinkles on the sunlit rose
And slithers from the thorn
Too slow to show the gun it knows
Is like a poisoned Pawn...
Her fire isn't in her kiss,
It isn't in her eyes;
I really shouldn't tell you this,
But something in her thighs
And hips above them lead me on
To reconstruct in dreams
The body her bikini's on—
Thematic as it seems!

'Jamie'

[forty—nine]

How many lines are lost on lust
For Edith or for Kate?
He puts his trust in cut and thrust,
In loving coming late—
To trade the *kibitzer* they drub,
The *patzer* out of place:
Is he a member of the club
They call the Human Race?
'Tis time to come down from the clouds,
Like ordinary men
To mingle with the single crowds—
Jehovah's Bill and Ben
Vociferating: "You're a god!"
To which concession sighs
As softly as a cotton wad
On which a fix relies.

'Tarryn'

[fifty]

A lamp has lit a losing soul
To prove it wasn't lost:
In prey to her, of grassy knoll
And hint of hillocks crossed,
I keep her card, with measurements
Another realm employs
Beyond my ken of pleasure—dense
Pretence for bigger boys!
True: she's a model, I am not,
Nor weigh up wannabes;
I do, however, think I've got
What for her pretty pleas
Might be of interest, offers that
Je ne sais quoi, you know:
If she's too sexy for her cat,
I'm Edgar Allan Poe!

'Drea'

[fifty-one]

She takes me to a party, partly
Proud but mostly meek,
Lest disappointment, losing heart,
Reveal, so to speak,
A lover she can't recognize—
The man who came to come,
To plumb the darkness 'twixt her thighs
Admissible to some...
She calls me *sweetheart*, just in case
I'm worthy of that jibe,
When all the time I must embrace
Her brothers' lustful tribe
Who cock their tails—left to watch,
I'm busted like a screw
They're driving into twilight's crotch
Less visible than true.

'Thomas'

[fifty-two]

If *T-Rex* took up *Genesis,*
He wasn't in a rush
To implicate his *nemesis*—
The hand he wants to crush
Resigns himself to Newton's *pomme,*
For *Everest* is why
'Tis harder still descending from,
Than conquering a lie...
The sharpest tool in any shed
Puts paid to my degrees—
To spell *finis*, as many wed
Disposable disease
To love I put my finger on,
Albeit he won't laugh,
Nor let a smile linger on
Obsession cut in half.

'Alva'

[fifty-three]

She grew up like a tender shoot
Acquainted well with grief—
No majesty to crown her root,
Except for whom belief
Comes quickly, as a cutlass whets
Obsidian: as my
Neuroses weave their mating nets
For those who go awry...
En prise are Kings and Queens who doff
Society of game,
Selecting Pawns for chopping off
Infinities of shame
Of which she has awoken much
Nocturnal lost-and-found,
As pundits pander to her touch—
Lest oddity compound!

'Sandra'

[fifty-four]

A butterfly, petite and true,
She's dancing in the light
For suitors mooted to be few—
At least in fancy's flight!
Parbleu! It seems I'm in the mix—
Or do I seld-deceive?
She sends me cards from Chamonix
Lest predilection grieve
For prehistoric shanty towns
Enamoured of her smile's
Meteoric hand-me-downs
Reputed to beguile
Comeliness to come for Kings
Whose Queens, ensconced above,
Surrender to immortal things—
Like moments lost to love.

'Boris'

[fifty-five]

When all in life is vanity
And striving after wind,
There's logic in your sanity
For prima donnas pinned—
Who love the Lord, as you applaud
Eternal beauty which
Redounds to both who take on board
The pallor and the pitch...
"He looks just like a movie star!"
Who? Some of us may pose
The question of Caïssa's Tsar:
Love's gentlemanly rose,
Who was a class above, below
Psychology's good moves—
As consolation's cameo
So eloquently proves!

'Pat'

[fifty-six]

Like royalty he wears pyjamas
To our local store—
If melodramas end in karma's
On-the-spot *rapport,*
I join him on his nature strip
In wonder *nonchalant*
To take his edict up and sip
The beer of *bons vivants...*
Such picture-perfect *bonhomie*!
Good Lord, I praise your mute
Endorsement of his colony—
His love affair and fruit:
For they walk straight, where others stray,
Amongst whom I am one—
Yet he makes love to yesterday
As though 'twere just begun.

'Eve'

[fifty-seven]

Impossibility—you are
Like ten-fold majesty
Commanding complications far
From *minnesong*-to-be...
Long time, no see—I'm like the dew
Infecting rose and bud;
Albeit liegemen link to you
Condolent lust for blood,
I'll court your breasts and crown your thighs,
I'll repossess your hips
To take the prize I catechize
With pulsing fingertips...
I say you are a goddess, though
My brethren say a fish
Came onto land—they oughta know,
But fervour lets me wish!

'Adam'

[fifty-eight]

To savour soul, then take its art
In naked lust for life,
Is like the bread we pull apart
And butter with his knife...
He's hungry—just don't give him fish,
Nor blood you say atones
For lust as black as liquorice,
The hooker in his bones...
She comes to him: no longer new,
She loves no little less
Than when desire in him drew
Psychotic nakedness
To sacrifice a boa's bind
For something within reach—
Not so unlike the way he dined
On love's precocious peach.

'Regina'

[fifty-nine]

The pieces are not many now
And Kings have lost their sheen—
But I shall love you anyhow,
My dear departed Queen!
If others think in groups, your danger's
Walking on the Moon—
So like a tigress for a stranger's
Militant cocoon,
You bare your fangs, if only then
To compensate for more
Rebuttals: to miff lonely men
Before they slam your door...
Must you resign? It's party time
As, blinded by delight,
The very Pawn they're scorning I'm
Promoting to a Knight!

'Paul'

[sixty]

The one whom I remember, still
Impressions on my mind,
Lends morning dew to sunlight's hill
Evocative and signed—
To see him smiling in my heart
In love not growing old
As we grow old, and grow apart
From hands to have and hold...
Jehovah, guide me, if thou wilt,
To be content in trust—
If brother God's not mine to jilt,
I, sparing juice and crust,
Can see a forest growing where
His wonder thought to wait
In witness borne to Kings who dare
To win, when Heaven's late.

Part Two:

"Let there be Joy..."

Sorority's Ad-Lib

Best of sisters, Alikat,
To bring, so Heaven-sent,
Relief for God's ole smelly rat,
Lest Hope, forever meant,

Dissolve like Aspirin, in a cup
Of water—to return
From whence tomorrow's Golden Pup
Purport to live, and learn...

For once upon an eon gone,
I'd glance into her crib,
And wish for Love to wait upon
Sorority's ad-lib.

'Sandy'

[sixty-one]

The first time ever, 'twas your tone
At which chimeras leapt—
As, errant in your combat zone,
Knights prepossessing wept...
Are you a square peg in a round
Holistic reverie?
I see you now, without a sound,
As tears incline to be—
So take these eyes, if I am blind
To golden hair I touch
Forsaken, evermore resigned
To be your *thought-as-much*
Residual: too singular
To make of us a word;
If things you are will bring you far
From me, I'm undeterred!

'Rach'

[sixty-two]

Is vengeance mine, if live I do,
In doing it so well?
If eloquence of soul is true,
Within her citadel
May lie, reclining, sure and chic,
A kitten in the sun,
Whose beauty purrs inside mystique
Atremble to outrun
The frolickers and fanciers
Left wailing in her wake—
Unable to entrance, be hers
Till death depart or take...
Now she is mine, in moments torn
From dreams I dare not broach,
Lest willingly I earn her scorn—
In love with her reproach.

'Fi Fi'

[sixty-three]

She's sitting pretty—up in smoke
What rumination chews;
And so 'tis mine, in awe, to poke,
With deft hullaballoos,
Her bubble: here in Eden's mall,
As yet not giving birth
To every creature great and small
Congesting Planet Earth,
Her symphonies of sympathy
Seek equilibrium:
Dear God, I'd let her tympani
Leak similes, become
Of souls entwined the enclave new,
As wet as winter grass
Of which the shock is is the dew
That nearly came to pass.

'Rocky'

[sixty-four]

Accuse him not of vagrancy,
Nor buckle him to beds;
His spirit settles fragrantly
Where unions hammer heads
And sickles suck the blooming life
From dandelions, in
Contempt of comrades grooming strife
For he who dares to win...
"I'm veak!" you *antebellum* play—
So who am I to coax
Quotations that, suffice to say,
Elaborate the hoax
Which you decline to disabuse
Of asterisk or star,
To leave to others, faking news,
Remorse for Shangri-La!

'Christian'

sixty-five

I pray to God—the one his cool
Philosophies disgrace;
I think, therefore I am a fool
Presenting Heaven's case:
The busyness of bees abuzz
With spring's contagious joy;
The ecstasy of Eden's fuzz
When Adam was a boy…
Yet he must counter x and y
To make the matter mute:
Theology he wrecks and I,
Illogical to boot,
Concede I'm just a *zygote*, too
Delusional to blame—
As Christian out of nothing grew,
Unworthy of the name!

'Shea'

[sixty-six]

Let winter coat her loveliness
With scarletry she pleads,
As I promote, from nothingness,
To something Heaven needs:
A man, to pass that tacit test
She's posing, not too late
To crown his *minne*'s asset, lest
He misconstrue a mate...
I'm dreaming of her craft at sea:
As feminine a boat
As ever won for mastery
Pre-eminence to float
On down before that Queen of yore
Without whom nights are glum—
For whom I'm wishing, lean and raw,
Her best is yet to come.

'Jane'

[sixty-seven]

Zut alors! Her souvenir's
Too beautiful to scan,
When eight as seven reappears—
As one, down to a man,
Embellishes her lonely page:
The strong and silent type
Is her raccoon, the only sage
She's forfeiting to hype...
Hey, Sister, why was six afraid
Of seven, eating nine?
Its strategy, so retrograde,
Like Heaven spilling wine,
Is catching on in couplets lent
When taxidermy's fools
Consider where their stuffing went—
As—*chic alors*!—she rules!

'Sash'

[sixty-eight]

Am I a Saint to let her be
Abuzz within my heart?
She's holier than letters we
Deconsecrate in art!
A relic worth a pittance I
Present to her content,
Yet never clinch admittance—why,
Must charity repent?
I'm just a simpleton, I know—
Comparative, at least,
To other sons she takes in toe
To soothe her savage beast:
And yet her holy spirit wins
Such sense from rich and poor
Inheriting, in pewter tins,
The key to Heaven's door.

'Dr No'

[sixty-nine]

A bind will bond men bound to be
Enamoured of that glow
Redounding to accountancy
He's mentoring—*chapeau*!
But Capa's dead! He loved in vain,
As Cuban as cigars
Corrupting, on that gravy train,
Unprincipled galahs!
A lover's lost, Caïssa's friend—
I just can't understand
How ties begin where fixtures end,
Minutiae at hand
To be, or not to be, renewed
Somewhere perhaps above:
Post vitam life is something you'd
Regret, if not for love.

'Mary'

[seventy]

Of someone's sacred heart she's boss:
Lord, let that heart be mine!
I shudder to believe her cross,
Her loaf inclined to whine—
Lest she, rerouting lees, so toast
My ham and cheese, to mate
Opinions with the uttermost
Proficiency I fête!
Dear God, why can't she be my dove?
I'd wash her webby feet!
Yes, verily I say, my love
Without her's incomplete—
For she may call me *Darling*, but
I know somebody else
Will bang her door at Christmas shut...
To jingle Heaven's bells!

'Ashleigh'

[seventy-one]

The smile which adorns her takes
Possession of my soul:
She's catering for ducks and drakes—
An egg and bacon roll
Comes with a coffee, flat and white,
On special: safe to say,
Whatever *lattes* won't requite
Espresso might—*au lait*!
Purrfection! I, amidst her toms,
Shall be comparative—
If she, superlative as bombs
Exploding, born to live
Forevermore inside my art,
Is absolute for one's
Apotheosis of that heart
So hot-to-trot with buns!

'Rose'

[seventy-two]

Your tears, if they must fall at all,
Are petals on my page:
The plover hears a mating call,
The heron's in a cage—
Where is your joy, the joy I'm owed?
I sing to you inside;
The lake I'm on, on which we rowed
Together, is too wide
To navigate with eyes ablur:
Forgive me, love in lieu
Of others somehow I incur,
Re-doing what they do—
When you complete this debtor's needs,
Your soul at sixty-four
So budding into life from seeds
Exquisitely at war.

'T-Swizzle'

[seventy-three]

The Holy Book with Heaven shook
In Paradise-to-be
For hangers on your tender hook—
First you, then I, then we...
Am I remiss to think you wise?
To think you where it's at?
I hear that you insure thighs
To feed your pussycat—
When love is lost for words to sing,
When hope has gone astray;
When butter's flying every spring
On heat that doesn't pay...
Still, in a fire, Fearless One,
I'd dance in my best suit—
Till you explore each cheerless pun
I fear I must recruit!

'Sally'

[seventy-four]

So far away—a Valentine
Too partisan to touch—
Albeit she's a pal of mine,
Or was: I thought as much!
So crystalline comes wit in streams
From lovely living lips—
To pit all my unwitting schemes
To get her giving hips
And toothpaste at a premium,
The gift of nuns, she claims,
Of which I buy the creamy sum
Gratuity defames...
A perfect ten? Her behemoth
Is adamant in faith—
If I were he, I'd cherish both
Anemone and wraith!

'Mandy'

[seventy-five]

A flower, be she Rose or Brooke,
Is lovely to my mind:
I think on her, to take a look,
And beauty's zenith find...
Sweet effervescence, crown her soul!
Chic loveliness, incline!
Indulgence, fold her in a stole
Embroidering her spine!
She isn't mine, her man's a mate,
Two craft for Lorelei
Are friendships, given her too late
To let me wonder why...
Tomorrow, as we lift our cups,
I'll tender her romance;
Whoever sniffs Love's buttercups
Is bound to charter chance!

'Elizabeth'

[seventy-six]

I'm sitting in a plane, a space
To segregate a gent,
When who should want to interface
Upon it, Heaven-sent,
But she: the steward comes to check
She's sixteen—that she is—
What, am I in a discotheque
Her pop may want to quiz?
It isn't mine to interfere,
T' engage her honeyed hue:
As lovely an external ear
As e'er, 'twixt me and you,
Enchantingly flew over seas
To be a miller's floss
Bequeathing Eden's grove, her knees
Beside him—at a loss!

'Jacinta'

[seventy-seven]

A rose—will ever wonders cease?
Shall I rewrite her hymn?
I'd make her face my frontispiece
And dedicate to whim
The lyricism in her, link
The spirit on her shelf—
If only, of an age to drink,
She'd brew it up herself...
Her beauty, so despotic, is
Exotic and humane;
Her writer, though neurotic, viz.
Robotic and inane,
May roll in clover brooking pet
Charades, to fall until
Her sunlight's overlooking, yet
Preponderating still!

'Frieda'

[seventy—eight]

Where is it gone? How can I spare
A dose of thee undone?
Be thou my vision, fit and fair
And foxier than fun
For love that didn't love, nor wed
Thy pleasant crescent ray
To moons aglow above a bed
Too taciturn to say...
Touché! Let nights to come arrive
And catch me in thy net,
Atremble just to be alive
By one so wan and wet:
For stars may jeer to find thee here
Caught unawares upon
The trail of a token tear
Embracing Heaven gone.

'Angela'

My wishful thinking pens a note:
Proposing, as you do,
Devotion for her petticoat—
And all that's under too!
But, mercy, she won't let me spread
My butter on her toast;
Where is the love her Jesus bled—
The prize she eyes the most?
How can it be? I'm making her
The answer to my prayer,
When I'm so unobservant: GUR—
That's *ground under repair*!
Good Lord, as love's my alibi,
I count on thee to make
The subject of my sally buy
The salt my cellars shake!

'Carti'

[eighty]

The person in your party dress
May give it added clout
If you forgive my tardiness
In taking beauty out
To places I had never seen
Preceding rooms for rent
Emboldening my evergreen
Devotion, as it went...
Let fire be your chaperone
'Neath skies you're bleeding red—
Desire is a compound loan
Until it goes to bed
To see the gallant in the good,
The moral in the mane,
Of half a mind to love as would
The Devil on my brain.

'Nicole'

[eighty-one]

The funeral is over now
But I'm not over you:
To let you die you must allow
A Heaven made for two—
The drops that fall, as though from clouds
Rebellious in love,
Are lost amidst the madding crowds
Alive but not above...
A penny for your thoughts? Shall I
Secrete your candle's glow?
Is sunset, like the knots they tie,
The dusk we had to know
Before the dawn of Paradise—
The touch ascension's hand
Bequeaths to mine? I sacrifice
A dove—then watch it land.

'Jak'

[eighty-two]

Of late I mate her tender likes
With loathing, it would seem,
For *up-and-comers*, swinging mics,
Who join her winning team
In *karaoke*—looking on
The woman, not the pearl,
Whose #1 intones *Dear John*
From just another girl...
In thinking of her, eyelids droop
As gloating ravens caw,
To cram a dais, *cock-a-hoop*
With hope she shows the door—
The hope once mine: Oh what a mess!
(The poem, not the way
Our truth's the life I gotta guess
Won't ask her to obey!)

'Gregor'

eighty-three

Of comedy the King, of love
The Matador in Flight;
Sir Walter, take your iron glove
And shake me with your might
That augurs well for good and fair,
The friends who claim your heart—
But who offends, less *debonair*,
Awaits a weather chart
Disquieting—for underneath
The mild-mannered cloak
Is lurking a volcano, sheath
Of lava I awoke
Deservedly: to take on board
The lessons verily
Ignored before Mt Etna roared
To life, *l'chaim*, free.

'Angel Fish'

[eighty-four]

Did you evolve, or were you sent
To Earth, the birth of Love?
Perhaps there is no argument—
Perhaps you, like a dove,
Must flutter down, Creation's Child,
Born to be my star:
If you must ever leave, your wild
Heart will bid *ta-ta*—
But in my own, so hollowed out,
No vision shall remain
Except the one my soul, devout,
Is left to entertain...
And that is you: the silken fur
They say from scales comes;
And, first of all, the pristine purr
A little angel hums.

'Anh'

[eighty-five]

He's waging war—to be the Lord
Is tempting, when you're not:
'Tis written Hiawatha thawed
Minnehaha, and got
Soccorso pronto for his heart
And healing for his soul,
Engaging love to love, each part
Revealing what it stole...
Christ Jesus, on your other hand,
So ardent is your flame—
Your gold is noble, getting panned
By quacks that, in your name,
In vain attempts to fix you up
Would pillory your pong
With jabs and tabs: a loving cup
Of Heaven, for the wrong.

'Max'

[eighty-six]

The looking glass I'm looking at
Is strewn with splattered fleas—
Of killing fields the diplomat
Am I: the Lord agrees...
How many wives do you propose
To pencil into pain?
How many aphids haunt the rose
You're fessing up to, slain?
So seeing, I take pains to squash
The very lease on life
I give to groom the face I wash
In existential strife...
And yet, if I (epitome
Of sinfulness in man)
Examine every bit of me,
I stumble on a fan!

'Freddy'

[eighty-seven]

So rich in peace—I, fiend defied,
Espy the gibbous Moon's
Extent, as your insecticide
Intones its merry tunes...
No man can ban petroleum—
Go ride your gypsy's bike
Art Deco as linoleum
Disposing must to like...
Oh what if we don't want you, cross
God's name off Heaven's list?
Sit! Good boy, listen to the Boss—
He's sober when he's... kissed!
I love your jeans, the way you dance—
Take Kelly and Astair
To boys in blue who chew your chants
You'd dust off bull to bare!

'Radha'

[eighty-eight]

She prays the days away, to risk
An answer, being wed
To worshipers she wins—who whisk
Her *will-o'-wisp* to bed,
And only then, subjecting her
To love they're making plain,
Concur astir with primal fur
So coarse and wet and vain...
Now pigeons in the morning coo
To promise Love Supreme
For deities like me and you
Gone sugaring her cream—
When forests black as char bewitch
Bamboozling belief
In countryside we tardy snitch
As in the night a thief.

'Gopal'

[eighty-nine]

You boo God's bobby on his beat,
As circumcision does,
But who's more *kosher* in defeat—
The felon or the fuzz?
Integrity's immutable—
It permeates like pain
Inside the body beautiful
Out forking in the rain...
Geronimo! He's coming down—
We're playing on a board
The same as game they're dumbing down
To obfuscate the Lord:
Who wins if He, downtrodden leaves
You trample underfoot,
Is reincarnate Love that weaves
Divinity through soot?

'Petal'

[ninety]

How shall I start? Her wild heart
Seconds complicit jaws
To pick apart inchoate art
With innocence she draws
Upon—to thrill a silent Knight
Reliant on a Mare
To help him hop in ells, alight
With fire-breathing air...
How can she know that, on the side,
His horse is bringing strife?
She's like a dove, his faithful guide,
If, weighing truth for life,
He's moving on: for one so great,
Let love itself demur;
How shall I end? In *tête-à-tête*
Forever—born to purr!

Part Three:

"Let there be Peace..."

She loves to love—sweet Princess G's
Felicity I pat
Adoringly, as if to squeeze
More Starlight from a cat †

Frère Jacques est amoureux:
Sa gentille Alouette chante
La danse d'un poème savoureux—
D'une beauté enchantée, savante †

It's time we see unraveling,
A skein of God's decree
She brews for lovers traveling,
And wilting—modestly †

I've loved you since the beginning of time,
My love for you, Dear, will grow anew, Dear,
Till the clocks of Eternity chime—
When they fall silent, we'll be in love, then...

'Ula'

[ninety-one]

You love her primal poise, as she,
The pearl at twenty-four,
Is elemental as the sea
Declining to be more:
She never saw an eagle fly
And never heard a pin
Until she caught your eagle eye
And felt it drop within;
Will she be nearly here in this
Calamity today?
Will you be left, the wind to kiss
And let her wish away?
Man is a liar, that we know,
And wars may never end
Till she sings little songs, as though
On fire for a friend.

'UI'

[ninety-two]

Now, is it only yesterday?
Of course—the day before's!
Albeit, settling west-away,
Heart's Kingdom's inner pause
Is able in a Dandelion's
Juniper in cloud
Ubiquitous—if man relies on
Sonnets we enshroud
Together, let me trade a case
Admitting voice and view,
Directing love to interface
On pedestals for two!
Revoke, if it so please, and I,
Evicting, shall impose,
Until the ends of never nigh,
Love's mem'ry, as it grows.

'Lida Garf'

ninety-three

Were loveliness to glove me less,
Why, kitten on my lap,
I'd settle like the Dove we bless
On cortices of sap...
Yet let not memes, to mention thee,
Conspire Hope for Grace
I sense envelop, spent on me,
Two links in time and space:
Momentum's angel—just assess
This quest yon fool and flood,
Encrypting thee, above redress,
Mere rumination's cud,
E'er mask in *minne* mine to muse
Upon, as in my heart
A mother maketh hymn a ruse
To enter thee... in art!

'Bud'

[ninety-four]

Behold this bloody silly git—
Or, adjutant to thine
Accession to the throne of wit:
Thy *buddy* killing rhyme!
Here's to that level palindrome
In far Glenelg we broach—
(Not eggy as a sally home
Engaging us to poach—)
Fan, let us go to bask on beaches:
Aliens in rows
Dispense with raiment, ripe as peaches
God in Heaven grows...
Remember Fathers, rest in peace
As others take a squiz—
Negotiating room for geese
To gander over his!

'Jo'

[ninety-five]

If I made itchy what, in guilt,
Considers me thy tizz—
Let ink not wonder why a quilt
Just isn't, or it is!
An olden soul, the Golden Bowl
Of Life, for someone wise—
Yet not for me: where is the knoll
On which I weep, to rise?
But once again doth enter dusk—
If morrows ought be true,
The one to hold my heart and husk
Might rend asunder new
Antipathy, to answer "Yes!"
And bleed as I have bled—
For worlds possessed of comeliness
Are better blushing red.

'Sophie'

[ninety-six]

Eternity, thought oh so short—was late:
Ere therelongfor a shell on me befête,
Veridity set in—a heavy weight...
Love's interstate: my clutterings were pack'd—
Methought her *tête-à-tête* the more forlack'd,
If aught in Wisdom's coveting a crate
Sophisticates of Devilry God's bait...
What, were my cards, like Hefeweizen, stack'd?

Then *she*, inside the train, ahead I felt
The melting velvet of two hearts inclined,
So kind, so quick—yet keen? Rewinding mind
I find her hope here in-between, re-dealt

Affinity's elective, song so true
Still kissing me inside, as if she knew.

'She's...'

[ninety-seven]

She's quiet—like a choir, musk

As missing as a lark

Who oughtn't get much higher: dusk

Before it's getting dark...

Tomorrow I may see her—yes,

But only if she's there;

As soothing as a paean, less

Confronting than a prayer...

She's hiding in the sockets, spots

Are distancing regret

Electrical as pockets—what's

More reason to forget...

I'm wishing like a washer she's

About to take a nap—

Lest Highest Heaven's posher keys

Compose her thunderclap!

'Yasmin'

[ninety-eight]

A row of roses tenders one
Elixir for my fix
In love begun, ere twilight done
Put sunshine in the mix...
She's eighteen now, not twice her age,
As high-fives she afflicts
On players ever game, contagious
Candles wan for wicks...
To spawn a thorny question: How
Am I to toc her tics?
As nettlesome an issue now
I'm nearly ripe for sticks—
Yet hope I'm holding out to ride
Her go-kart, skirting slicks
Unsettling boy and man inside:
Am I the One she nicks?

'Katiča'

[ninety-nine]

Where what was White is Black a while,
Enter loving Greys—
An even ally, back in style,
Lastingly conveys
The thought there maybe might be hope
Heroic, on the way:
Good manners over *manna*, *mammon*'s
Otiose purée...
Now, if she comes, my heart must leap
Eternally to roam
Where water wells with salt to weep
Her Wisdom, coming home—
Yon threshold to cross over—cats!—
Sweet Paris Chloë Rose
Is Katswold Blackie's pool of pats'
Nobility... she glows!

'You'

[one-hundred]

You love me back—in subterfuge?
I join your polka dots
Impatiently, to splutter *rouge*
On non-existent spots...
You bat a lid and lift a lobe—
So who am I to wax
On this old turning, trembling globe
In love but one attracts?
For combinations procreate
Free space for more than two
Mistakes it takes to ovulate
In rooms without a view:
How can I see your canopy
Inside—too Black to win
The Knight, whose lyric panoply
Extends what you begin!

'Farruġ'

[one—hundred—one]

Howbeit knowing thee, yet somehow not—
I wish I would, yet someone's something could—
My heart, so crusty, shaken, shorn the shot—
Might come to speak as stiff as balsawood—
Even ken, attractive in a—wait: I
Look at her, and she looks back—at what?

Upuntil season's end, if England snow—
Nigh was it in the days of long ago—
Dew coming on the leaves, lest sunlight's toe
Hop Eros into Psyche's quest yon flow—
O Lord sweet Byron, Tennyson's *propos*,
No better—best! Just in his candle's glow...

I grow: "Be not afraid, to do it slow"—
Gone with the Dragon's kite, *adagio*...

'Chrissie'

[one-hundred-two]

I won her welcome, sang her dues,
And, every time I come,
Miraculously crossing bruise
And pandemonium,
Necessities confine me here—
On her I think again
To see the one whose eyes, so clear,
Herodotus would pen...
Evict conviction—how am I
Repudiating sense?
Frequent the sky, if thou must fly
Reluctantly immense:
In wise to weigh up how I cheat
Exception—like a rope
No less than Heaven's Paraclete
Doth twine for me, in hope.

'Claire'

[one-hundred-three]

She flitters in, she flutters by—
My *papillon de nuit*
Might settle 'twixt the shutters I
Foreclose, to better see
Demure, clear, her passion dear
Slow dancing through the storm
Of yesterdays no longer near—
Too tremulous and warm
To steal away, as flames purvey,
On wicks of haematite,
The love she's saving for the play
Of acumen, and light...
Thus thither, on her pilgrim's trek,
By her I must abide—
To trade a lover's *szeretlek*
For pieces of my bride.

'David'

[one-hundred-four]

Atop a hill, there in the road,
A shining five-cent piece
Despicable as Satan's load
To whom it gives release...
He sees it, promptly turns for home,
The fortune in his head
Still legal tender—for in Rome
What's Caesar's, in the Red,
Belongs to Caesar: Black is only
Blood in David's veins,
Prising with a chisel lonely
Heartlight that disdains...
What can I add? My dear old Dad
Is better off below
The sod that makes a flower mad—
And hesitant to grow.

'Szabóné'

A lover, on parade for you,
D'Artagnan righting wrongs,
Surrenders serenades in lieu
Of syndicating songs
You're dancing to: remote, divine,
You brook a lion's roar
Above so many serpentine,
So ill-equipped to soar,
The bold, the brave, the brilliant seas
Inspiriting the swift
Accomplice of his sylvan breeze
Which longs for love to lift
And chauffeur you, if faith know how,
Productive in address
He's taking off—you pray: "Go now,
Before I acquiesce..."

'Philip'

[one-hundred-six]

Is loveliness my brother? We
Were friends before I knew—
Who waits on love as verily
Love wakes inside of you?
So gentle to the spirit, no
Less beautiful to view:
You're letting me re-stirrup, so
I'm doing it for two...
A heart as boundless as the sky,
Your four-leaf clover grew,
And rising, though I don't know why,
In sunshine mine to woo,
Made mystery of succour, man—
How can it be so true?
The tic and toc, how time began
Beginnings in the dew.

'Shrī Shrī'

[one-hundred-seven]

Eternity—your letters, eight,
Persisting from the start
Of time: his ever verdant mate
Adjourning in a heart
Acquainted well with loneliness
Until he came across
The fragrance of your loveliness—
A dire albatross
Takes solace in a tender swift
Through dreams he hopes to lose
Inside desire set adrift
From love too hard to choose...
King Solomon, dost covet wings
More precious than a stone?
You lost her ruby—paper rings
Requite her lustre thrown!

'Bobby-Jim'

[one-hundred-eight]

I thank you, Lord; I love you back:
The White King and His Knight
Criss-cross in *szeretlek*-attack,
As well you'd think they might...
But Darkness on the Edge of Town
Is brewing up morose
Myopia—bring on the Clown
Enchantingly verbose
In prayers we daren't see in cars
Abandoning the bog
For mixing cocktails into bars
As Phileas as fog:
Authentic to more eyes undone
By fifty years' deceit
Than Pentateuch's lore—why fun won
With nothing left to cheat.

'The Foe'

[one—hundred—nine]

Let every Eva love you, come and go

With *Ludwig van* on single-digit seas,

As, row on row, *ailurophobic* grow

The prayers you bark at Mary, on the breeze...

Roll over, God, how do you keep it up?

When you were just a child, someone cried;

A shepherd isn't guilty as a pup,

So love you lost, and, living it, you lied...

If truth will set you free, uncage a soul

Where constant come the cries to be let out;

As 'twas in the beginning, like a Pole

Exacting vengeance on a sour Kraut,

You're going for the record—go for yields

You owe to all the dead, in Flanders Fields.

'The Lion'

[one—hundred—ten]

The Lion's King, and so may well appear
The Lord of jungle, jingle, jam, and juice:
But what's that in his eye—a lonely tear?
His majesty's a vacuous caboose!
He's like a hiker holding out a thumb
For whom no heart will stop—despotic rants
Give way to rosy seas of kindred crumbs
Begetting an eternal second chance...
But grace is slow, his fall from it complete—
In royal games he's taking on the chin,
Catastrophes, in imminent defeat
Compete with pride, as he, condemned to win,

Pretends to love, as lionesses burn
To kiss his whiskers—sorry to be stern.

Jade, for love of thee, I pen
A paean to thy soul;
For, if I wish to, that is when
Subservient my rôle
Will pry on thee—the best of men,
If such I am, who stole
Thine image, hoping, yet again,
T' envisage Heaven's knoll...
Wherefore art thou, Love divine,
So radiant and true,
To sip on, like Jehovah's wine
A pilgrimage on dew—
Such progress for the aquiline
In me, for whom I knew
That beauty borne from such as thine
Shall make of lovers two

Hearts melting on an open stage:
The Lord Primeval, Jade's to cage.